ΤΟ ΑΞΙΟΝ ΕΣΤΙ

✤

THE AXION ESTI

An International Poetry Forum Selection

Translated and Annotated by

EDMUND KEELEY and GEORGE SAVIDIS

ΟΔΥΣΣΕΑ ΕΛΥΤΗ

ΤΟ ΑΞΙΟΝ ΕΣΤΙ

✤

THE AXION ESTI

ODYSSEUS ELYTIS

UNIVERSITY OF PITTSBURGH PRESS

For Mary and Lena,

who first brought the translators together

Library of Congress Catalog Card Number 79-49274
ISBN 0-8229-5318-8

"The Genesis" is reprinted, in slightly revised form, from *Poetry,* © October 1964 by The Modern Poetry Association, and appears here by permission of the Editor of *Poetry.* An earlier translation of "The Gloria" was first published in *Agenda,* Winter 1969, and is reprinted by permission of the Editor.

Edmund Keeley expresses his gratitude to the John Simon Guggenheim Memorial Foundation for assisting him with a grant during the preparation of this translation.

Publication of this book has been made possible by a grant

from Tasso and Jane Katselas

and by a special grant

from the Greek Orthodox Archdiocese

of North and South America

in memory of His Holiness Patriarch Athenagoras I.

Πλεονάκις ἐπολέμησάν με ἐκ νεότητός μου,

καὶ γὰρ οὐκ ἠδυνήθησάν μοι.

ΨΑΛΜΟΣ ΡΚΗ

Many a time have they afflicted me from my youth:

yet they have not prevailed against me.

PSALM 129:2

CONTENTS

FOREWORD

The hope of the International Poetry Forum is to be no less international than poetry itself. To be sure, such a hope invites certain practical limitations. While poetry has the destiny of speaking to all men at all times, the International Poetry Forum concerns itself with bringing particular poets into contact with as many people as possible right now. While poetry speaks ultimately from and to the common nationality of flesh and blood, the International Poetry Forum attempts in a proximate way to permit poets of different nationalities and alphabets to have their work known and understood by people of nationalities and alphabets other than their own.

To help achieve this goal the International Poetry Forum has initiated a series of foreign selections. These selections provide for the publication of American translations of some of the works of foreign poets and the distribution of such books throughout the United States, Europe, and the poets' homelands.

The Axion Esti by Odysseus Elytis, which has been named by poets and Greek scholars alike as one of the major Greek poems of this century, is the seventh in this series, the first six having been the Turkish Selection (*Selected Poems* by Fazıl Hüsnü Dağlarca, translation by Talât Halman) in 1968; the Syria-Lebanon Selection (*The Blood of Adonis* by Adonis, or Ali Ahmed Said, translation by Samuel Hazo) in 1971; the Swedish Selection (*Windows and Stones* by Tomas Tranströmer, translation by May Swenson) in 1972; the Israeli Selection (*A Canopy in the Desert* by Abba Kovner, translation by Shirley Kaufman) in 1973; the Jamaican Selection (*Uncle Time* by Dennis Scott) in 1973; and *Eskimo Poems from Canada and Greenland* (translation by Tom Lowenstein) in 1974.

SAMUEL HAZO, *Director*
International Poetry Forum

PREFACE

Odysseus Elytis, who first established his reputation as a gifted lyricist in the late thirties and early forties, ended more than a decade of silence with the publication of *The Axion Esti* in December 1959. The poem, clearly his most ambitious work to that date and since, earned a mixed reception from Greek critics when it first appeared and still remains a subject of controversy. Nevertheless, it earned the First National Award for Poetry in 1960 and became one of the most widely read volumes of verse to have appeared in Greece since World War II (now in its seventh edition) and a continuing favorite among younger readers of poetry.

The Axion Esti can perhaps be taken best as a kind of spiritual autobiography which attempts to dramatize the national and philosophical extensions of a highly personal sensibility. The poet's strategy —reminiscent of Whitman's in *Song of Myself* and Sikelianos's in *Prologue to Life*—is to present an image of the contemporary Greek consciousness through the developing perspective of a first-person persona who is at once the poet himself and the voice of his country. The first section of the poem, "The Genesis," depicts the birth and growing awareness of this half-mythical first person as it comes to know "this small world the Great"; the second section, called "The Passion," focuses on the persona's less innocent experience of World War II and its tragic aftermath; the third section, "The Gloria," celebrates in a long hymn of praise the sensual and spiritual vitality the enlightened persona finds in the world that still remains open to him after he has gained the knowledge of human evil and human sacrifice in his country's recent history.

The pervasive theme of the poem is that the measure of man's humanity resides in his ability to hold opposites in just relation, his ability to survive as neither angel nor devil, sensualist nor saint, but as something beyond the two, something that can assimilate both. What most clearly defines the contemporary Greek sensibility, it would seem, is its capacity for balancing the world of the senses and the world of the spirit. The surviving consciousness the persona represents is that which can see the holiness, the "forever," even in ephemeral objects and sensations that are rooted in Elytis's "small world the Great."

In each of the three sections, the "autobiographical" elements—

xi

those having to do with the growth of the poet's imagination and knowledge in response to the felt life around him—are colored constantly by allusion to the historical and literary tradition of Greece. Elytis's sources range from Homer and Heraclitus to the Byzantine hymnographers, the demotic poets of the nineteenth century, and the surrealist poets of the twentieth century. And his evocation of contemporary history—especially that of the Albanian campaign, the German occupation, and the civil war in "The Passion"—continually echoes the earlier history of the Turkish occupation and the War of Independence. The same attempt to identify the contemporary consciousness with its antecedents in the Greek tradition determines the form and style of the poem in a number of places. The tone, diction, and structure of individual segments often reflect parts of the Greek Orthodox liturgy, and there are passages in the poem that deliberately echo folk songs, the poems and prose of Solomos, or the memoirs of General Makriyannis. But the controlling voice throughout remains that of a mature Elytis, sometimes self-indulgent, sometimes grandiloquent, but generally singing out the surrealist lyricism of his early verse in a purified, elevated form that reveals new power and depth.

The problems of rendering a voice so rich in traditional echoes alien to English and so subjectively rhetorical are unusually acute. We have tried to diminish one inevitable form of distortion by not attempting to duplicate the intricate formal patterns of some of the lyrics in "The Passion," though we do offer a metrical equivalent of Elytis's loose tetrameter in "The Gloria." We have also resisted—with a few exceptions—the temptation to use the idiom and tone of the King James Version of the Bible in rendering passages influenced by the Greek Orthodox liturgy, which is not at all "biblical" in ways parallel to a Jacobean text. On the other hand, we have tried to find a relevant English parallel for the earthy nineteenth-century demotic in several of the "Readings" in "The Passion." Generally, our aim throughout the poem has been to create a rhetorical equivalent that sounds natural and contemporary in English, even if sometimes a bit abstract or hyperbolic by comparison to the language normal to poetry in the English-speaking world since Pound and Eliot and Auden established what has become the contemporary idiom in their tradition. To deny Elytis his flourishes and hyperboles would be to translate him dishonestly (as would be true of a Greek translator rendering, say, Dylan Thomas). At the same time, we have to acknowledge that any mode of translating poetry that depends so heavily on the resources of sound, rhythmic change, and localized idiom is certain to do the original one kind of injustice or another. We have chosen what we take to be the lesser of possible evils by not presuming to offer our own arbitrary and foreign patterns of sound, rhythm, or idiom in a doomed effort to imitate the Greek poet more or less literally.

The first and third sections of this translation have been somewhat revised since their publication, respectively, in *Poetry* (October 1964) and *Agenda* (Winter 1969). "The Passion" is published here for the first time. Our work on this section was assisted in the first instance by Amy Mims, who provided us with a helpful version and who should be regarded as a silent collaborator in preparing our earliest draft of this section. We also found useful hints in the version presented by George Niketas as a doctoral dissertation at the University of Georgia (*DA*, 1967: 67–16235), which also provides a commentary on the poem and extensive notes. Further critical commentary can be found in the issue of *Poetry* mentioned above, in *To Axion Esti tou Elyti (The Axion Esti of Elytis)* by Tassos Lignadis (Athens, 1971), and particularly in an article by Professor D. N. Maronitis in *Epoches*, September 1965. The Greek edition of *The Axion Esti* is not annotated, but the poet has written a detailed commentary for private use. Our notes here, based in part on this commentary, are intended to provide only the kind of information that may prove particularly helpful to the English reader of the poem, and this without pretension to critical interpretation.

Athens, Greece   EDMUND KEELEY
July 1973   GEORGE SAVIDIS

THE GENESIS

IN THE BEGINNING the light And the first hour

      when lips still in clay

      try out the things of the world

  Green blood and bulbs golden in the earth

  And the sea, so exquisite in her sleep, spread

  unbleached gauze of sky

  under the carob trees and the great upright palms

      There alone I faced

      the world

      wailing loudly

My soul called out for a Signalman and Herald

      I remember seeing then

      the three Black Women

  raising their arms toward the East

  Their backs gilded, and the cloud they were leaving behind

  slowly fading

      to the right And plants of other shapes

  It was the sun, its axis in me

  many-rayed, whole, that was calling And

the One I really was, the One of many centuries ago

the One still verdant in the midst of fire, the One still tied to heaven

      I could feel coming to bend

      over my cradle

And his voice, like memory become the present,

assumed the voice of the trees, of the waves:

      "Your commandment," he said, "is this world

      and it is written in your entrails

      Read and strive

      and fight," he said

"Each to his own weapons," he said

And he spread his hands as would

a young novice God creating pain and mirth together

  First the Seven Axes, wrenched with force,

  pried loose from high up in the battlements,

  fell to the ground

                         as in the great Storm
                         at its zero point
                         where a bird gives forth its fragrance
                         from the beginning again
       the blood was homing clean
       and the monsters were taking on a human shape
                              So very manifest, the Incomprehensible
            Then all the winds of my family arrived too
            the boys with puffed-out cheeks
            and tails green and broad, mermaidlike
                              and others, old men: familiar, ancient
                              shell-skinned, bearded
             And they parted the cloud in two, and these again into four
             and what little remained they blew away, chasing it off to the North
             With broad foot and proudly, the great Tower tread the waters
       The line of the horizon flashed
       so visible, so dense and impenetrable

                         THIS the first hymn.

       AND THE ONE I really was, the One of many centuries ago,
       the One still verdant in the midst of fire, the One not made by human hand,
                              drew with his finger the distant
                              lines
              sometimes rising sharply to a height
              sometimes lower: the curves gentle
                              one inside the other
       land masses that made me feel
       the smell of earth like understanding
                         So real it was
                         that the earth followed me faithfully
              becoming redder in secret places
              and elsewhere full of tiny pine needles

                              4

Then, more nonchalantly,
                        the hills, the slopes,
and later, with the hand slowly in repose,
                        the valleys, the plains,
        and again, suddenly, rocks wild and barren
those of forceful impulses
        He stopped a moment to ponder things
                        difficult or lofty:
                        Olympus, Taygetus were born
                        "Something that will stand by you
                        even after your death," he said
        And he drew thread through the stones
        and brought forth slate from the entrails of the earth
        laid broad steppingstones all around the slope
        There, alone, he placed
                        white marble fountains
                        mills of wind
                        tiny pink cupolas
                        and tall perforated dovecotes

Virtue with its four right angles
And since he thought it beautiful for each to be in another's arms
        the large watering troughs filled with love
        the cattle lowered their heads gently, calves and cows
        as though the world held no temptations
        as though knives were yet unknown
"To endure peace you need strength," he said
        and swinging around with palms open he sowed
                        mullein, crocuses, bluebells
                        all variety of earthly stars
        and cut into one leaf of each, as a mark of their origin,
                        their superiority and strength:

THIS WORLD
this small world the great!

5

BUT BEFORE hearing the wind or music
as I was setting out to find a vista
(climbing a boundless red sand dune
erasing History with my heel)
I wrestled with my bed sheets What I was looking for was this,
innocent and tremulous like a vineyard
deep and unscarred like the sky's other face,
A drop of soul amidst the clay
Then he spoke and the sea was born
And I gazed upon it and marveled
In its center he sowed little worlds in my image and likeness:
Horses of stone with manes erect
and tranquil amphorae
and slanting backs of dolphins
Ios, Sikinos, Serifos, Milos
"Each word a swallow
to bring you spring in the midst of summer," he said
And ample the olive trees
to sift the light through their fingers
that it may spread gently over your sleep
and ample the cicadas
which you will feel no more
than you feel the pulse inside your wrist
but scarce the water
so that you hold it a God and understand the meaning of its voice
and the tree alone
no flock beneath it
so that you take it for a friend
and know its precious name
sparse the earth beneath your feet
so that you have no room to spread your roots
and keep reaching down in depth
and broad the sky above
so that you read the infinite on your own

THIS WORLD
this small world the great!

6

"AND THIS WORLD you must see and receive,"

      he said: Look! And my eyes sowed the seed

      racing faster than rain even

      over a thousand virgin acres

Sparks taking root in darkness and sudden jets of water

                 I was clearing the silence to plant

                 seeds of phonemes and golden shoots of oracles

The hoe still in my hand

      I saw the great short-legged plants, turning their faces

      some barking, others sticking out their tongues

                 There the asparagus, there the kale

                 there the curling parsley

                 acanthus and dandelion

                 liatris and fennel

Secret syllables through which I strove to utter my identity

"Good," he said, "you know how to read

and you'll come to learn a great deal

      if you study the Insignificant in depth

      And the day will come when you take on helpers

                 Remember:

                 the hand-combatant Zephyr, the dark-destroying

                                pomegranate

                 the flaming fleet-footed kisses"

And his words disappeared as though perfume

Partridgelike, nine o'clock flushed toward the deep heart of euphony

                 the houses stood in solidarity

                 small and square

                 arches white and doors the color of bluing

    Under the trellised vines

    I mused for hours

    with the tiniest twittering

    with croaking, chirping, distant cooing:

                 There the stork and pelican

                 there the turtledove

                 there the mallard and the owl

    And the mite was there too

    and what they call the Virgin's mare

The shore with my thighs naked to the sun

and two the seas on either side
of a third in-between: lemon, lime, and orange trees
and that northwest wind with the high strait confronting it
altering the sky's ozone

          Low down on the seafloor of the leaves
          the smooth gravel
          the tiny ears of the flowers
          and the impatient shoots which are really

THIS WORLD
this small world the great!

THEN I came to understand the seabreeze and the long endless whisper of the trees
    I saw the red jugs lined up on the quay
    and closer to the wooden shutter
    where I lay sleeping on my side
          the north wind crowed louder
          And I saw
Maidens beautiful and naked and smooth like pebbles
with that touch of black in the delta of the thighs
and that abundant, luxurious spread of it along the shoulderblades
          some upright sounding the Conch
          others spelling out in chalk
          words strange and enigmatic:
    ROES, ESA, ARIMNA
    NUS, MIROLTAMITY, YELTIS
          the small cries of birds and hyacinths
          or some other language of July
At the stroke of eleven
    five fathoms deep
    perch, goby, seabream
    with huge gills and short rudder tails
          Rising higher, I found

sponges and starfish
and slender, silent anemones
and higher still, at the water's lip
rose limpets
and half-open mussels and algae
"Precious names," he said, "ancient oaths
saved by Time and the sure ear of the distant winds"
And close to the wooden shutter
where I lay sleeping on my side
I pressed the pillow tight against my chest
and my eyes filled with tears
I was in the sixth month of my love
and in my entrails stirred a precious seed

THIS WORLD
this small world the great!

"BUT FIRST you will see the wilderness and give it your own meaning," he said
"The wilderness will precede your heart
and then again the wilderness will follow it
Know this above all:
whatever you salvage under lightning
will remain pure eternally"
And high above the waves
he set up villages of rocks
There the foam arrived as dust
I saw a lean goat licking the crevices
its eye slanted, its sparse body hard as quartz
I lived through the locusts and the thirst and the rough-jointed fingers
for the fixed number of years ordained by the Wise
Bent over papers and bottomless books
climbing down them on a slender rope
night after night

9

I sought whiteness to the utmost intensity
of blackness, hope to the point of tears
joy to the outer limit of despair

  The moment was designated for help to be sent
  and the task was allotted the rains

      rivulets sang the day long
      I ran madly

on the slopes I tore terebinth, my palm gave myrtle freely
to the breeze's bite

  "That's purity," he said, "It is
  the same on the slopes as in your entrails"

  And he spread his hands as would

an old experienced God creating clay and heavenliness together
He heated the peaks barely red

  and nailed the grass — green, unnibbled — onto the ravines

      mint, lavender, verbena
      and the small hoof prints of sheep

or again elsewhere, falling from the heights
light threads of silver, cool hair of a girl I saw and wanted

      Tangible woman

      "Purity," he said, "is she"

  and full of yearning I caressed the body
  kisses teeth to teeth; then one inside the other

      Storm-tossed
      like a cape I trod so deeply
      that air surged into the caves

Like a white-sandaled echo the gar
passed fleetingly below the water's surface

  and high above, having the hill for a foot and the sun for a horned head
  I saw the great Ram climbing the air

And the One I really was, the One of many centuries ago
the One still verdant in the midst of fire, the One still bound to heaven

      whispered when I asked

What is Good? What is Evil?:
"A point A point

  and on it you find balance and exist
  and beyond it turmoil and darkness

10

and before it the roar of angels
A point A point
and on it you can progress infinitely
otherwise, nothing else exists any more"
And the Scales which, stretching my arms,
seemed to balance light and instinct, were

THIS WORLD
this small world the great!

BECAUSE THE HOURS turned like days
with broad violet leaves on the garden clock
I became the dial
Tuesday   Wednesday   Thursday
June   July   August
I showed a need that now struck me full-faced
like brine The girls insects
Distant flashings of the Rainbow —
"All this is the time of innocence
the time of the cub and green shoots
a time long before Necessity," he said
And he prodded danger with his finger
And he placed a black eyebrow on the ridge of the cape
From an unknown source he poured out phosphorus
"So you may see," he said
"within your body
veins of potassium, manganese
and the calcified
ancient remnants of love"
And then my heart shuddered
it was the first creak of wood inside me
the hooting of a night

11

                    perhaps approaching
                                        the blood of someone killed
                                        returning to the upper world
                    Far beyond, at my soul's edge
                                        I saw secretly passing by
tall farming lighthouses On the precipices, close-hauled castles
The polar star Saint Marina with the demons
                    And farther still, beyond the waves
                    on the Island gulfed by olive groves
                    it seemed for a moment that I saw Him
                    He who gave his blood to make me flesh
                    ascending the thorny path of the Saint
                                        once again
                                        Once again
                    I saw him touch his fingers to the waters of Yera
                    and light the five villages
                                        Papados   Plakados   Paleokipos
                                        Skopelos   Messagros
                    inheritance and dominion of my clan
"But now," he said, "your other face
must rise to the light"
                    and long before my mind saw
                    a sign of fire or sepulchral shape
                                        he turned toward that which no one else could see
                                        and bending
                                        with his hands thrust forward
                                        he prepared the great Voids on earth
                                        and in man's body:
the void of Death for the Coming Infant
the void of Murder for Just Judgment
the void of Sacrifice for Equal Compensation
the void of the Soul for Responsibility Toward Others
                                        And Night, the violet
                                        of an ancient Moon
                                        sawed through by nostalgia
with the ruins of an abandoned windmill and the blameless fragrance of excrement,
                                        found a place inside me

                                        12

changed the dimensions of faces, distributed weight in new ways
My hard body was the anchor dropped among men
      where there is no other sound
                but that of dead thuds, wailing and lamentation
                crevices on the upturned face
The scion of what nonexistent race I might be
      I knew only then
                as the notion of Others
                oblique like the edge of glass
                cut me straight and clean through
      I saw into houses clearly, as though they had no walls
      old women went by, oil lamps in their hands
      lines on their foreheads and on the ceiling
and other young men, moustached, arming their belts
                silent
                two fingers on the hilt
                centuries now.
"You see," he said, "they are the Others
and it cannot be They without You
nor can it be You without Them"
"You see," he said, "they are the Others
                and you must face them without fail
if you want your image to be indelible
                and remain what it is
      Because many are those who wear the black shirt
      and others speak the language of porcupines
      and there are the Raw-eaters and the Water-brutes
      the Bread-fearers and the Leadenfaced and the Neocondors
      the herd and multitude at the cross corners
                of the Tetractys"
"If you can really bear to face them," he said,
"your life will shape to a point and you will lead," he said
                "Each to his own weapons," he said
And the One I really was, the One of many centuries ago
the One still verdant in the midst of fire, the One still bound to heaven
                entered into me, became
                the one I am

At three o'clock in the morning
    above the shacks, distant
        the first cock crowed
For a second I saw the Upright Pillars, the Metope of Powerful Beasts
    and Men bringing Knowledge of God
The Sun assumed its face, the Archangel forever on my right

      THIS I then
      and the small world the great!

THE PASSION

I

HERE then am I,
created for the young Korai and the Aegean islands,
lover of the deer's leaping,
initiate in the Mystery of olive leaves,
sun-drinker and locust-killer.
Here am I, face to face
with the black shirts of the ruthless
and of the years' empty belly that aborted
its own children, in heat!
Wind releases the elements and thunder assaults the mountains.
Fate of the innocent, alone again, here you are in the Straits!
In the Straits I opened my hands.
In the Straits I emptied my hands
and saw no other riches, heard no other riches
but cool fountains running,
Pomegranates or Zephyr or Kisses.
Each to his own weapons, I said:
In the Straits I'll open my pomegranates.
In the Straits I'll post Zephyrs as sentries,
I'll unleash the old kisses canonized by my longing!
Wind releases the elements and thunder assaults the mountains.
Fate of the innocent, you are my own Fate!

GREEK the language they gave me;
poor the house on Homer's shores.
>My only care my language on Homer's shores.
There bream and perch
>windbeaten verbs,
green sea currents in the blue,
>all I saw light up in my entrails,
sponges, jellyfish
>with the first words of the Sirens,
rosy shells with the first black shivers.
>My only care my language with the first black shivers.
There pomegranates, quinces,
>swarthy gods, uncles and cousins
emptying oil into giant jars;
>and breaths from the ravine fragrant
with osier and terebinth
>broom and ginger root
with the first chirping of finches,
>sweet psalms with the very first Glory Be to Thee.
My only care my language with the very first Glory Be to Thee!
>There laurel and palm leaves
censer and incense
>blessing the swords and muskets.
On soil spread with vine-scarves,
>the smell of roasting lamb, Easter eggs cracking,
and "Christ is Risen,"
>with the first salvos of the Greeks.
Secret loves with the first words of the Hymn.
>My only care my language with the first words of the Hymn!

a

MY MOUTH *still in clay, yet it named you —*
Rosy, newborn babe, mottled first dew —
And since then, deep in daybreak, it shaped for you
The line of lips, the smoke of hair,
Gave you articulation, gave you the L and the Y,
The airy infallible stride.

And from that very moment, opening inside me
An unknown prison, gray and white birds
Rose bickering in the air, and I felt
Yours the blood and the tears,
The eternal strife, horrible and magnificent,
Yours the lure and the beauty.

In the woodwind of the trees and the ancient war dance clashing
Spears and swords, I heard You utter
Secret commands of a virginal life,
Words with the radiance of green stars,
And swinging over the abyss I saw and knew
"The terrible edge of your sword!"

THE MARCH TOWARD THE FRONT

AT DAYLIGHT on St. John's, the day after Epiphany, we got our orders to move up to the front again, out there where you don't find weekdays or holidays. We were to take over the line the Artans had been holding till then, from Khimara to Tepeleni. The reason being they'd been fighting since the first day, without a break, and only about half of them were left and they couldn't take it any longer.

Twelve whole days we'd been back there, in the villages. And just as our ears were again getting used to the sweet creaking of the earth and just as we'd begun gingerly to make sense out of a dog's barking or the clang of a distant church bell, they tell us we have to go back to the only sound we really knew: the slow and heavy cannon, the dry and quick machine guns.

Night after night we trudged ahead without stopping, one behind the other, like the blind — sweating to pull our feet out of the mud, sometimes in it up to our knees. Because it was usually drizzling out there on the road, just as it was inside us. And the few times we'd pull up for a rest, not a word, everyone serious and silent, we'd share our raisins one by one under the light from a bit of pine kindling. Or sometimes, when we got the chance, we'd rip off our gear and scratch ourselves wildly until we drew blood. Cause the lice were up to our ears, and that was even harder to take than being tired. Finally, through the darkness you'd hear a whistle signaling us to move out, and we'd push off again like pack animals to gain ground before daylight, when we'd make an open target for the airplanes. Because God didn't know about targets and things, so he'd stick to his habit of making the light come up at the same time every day.

Then, hidden in the ravines, we'd lay our heads down on the heavy side, the one that doesn't give out dreams. And the birds would get mad at us, thinking we weren't taking their talk very seriously — and maybe also because we were disfiguring nature for no reason. We were farmers of a different kind, carrying picks and tools of a different kind, damn them.

Twelve whole days back there in the villages we'd gazed for hours on end at the shape of our faces in the mirror. And just as our eyes were getting used again to the old familiar features, and just as we'd begun gingerly to make sense of the bare upper lip or the sleep-filled cheek, they tell us we have

20

to move, so that by the second night we began to feel we were changing again, more so by the third, until on the last, the fourth, it was clear we were no longer the same. Except it seemed we were marching along like a gang made up of all generations and ages, some from now and some from ancient times, turned white by too much beard. Scowling mountain chieftains with their headbands, tough priests, sergeants from the wars of '97 and '12, grim pioneers swinging their axes, Byzantine border guards with their maces and shields still covered with the blood of Turks and Bulgars. Together, no one speaking, groaning on side by side numberless years, crossing mountain ridges and the gorges between, no thought about anything else. Because just as people who get the bad breaks again and again become used to Evil and end up changing its name to Destiny or Fate, so we kept heading straight ahead for what we called the Plague, as we might have said the Fog or the Cloud — sweating to pull our feet out of the mud, sometimes in it up to our knees. Because it was usually drizzling out there on the road, just as it was inside us.

That we were very near the place where you don't find weekdays or holidays, sick people or healthy people, poor or rich, we now knew. Because the roar ahead, like a storm beyond the mountains, kept growing, so that in the end we could clearly read the slow and heavy cannon, the dry and quick machine guns. Also because more and more we started coming across the slow procession of the wounded, heading out the other way. And the medics, with the red cross on their arm bands, would set their stretchers down and spit on their hands, eyes wild for a cigarette. And when they'd hear where we were going, they'd shake their heads and start their tales of blood and terror. But we, the only thing we listened to were those other voices rising in the darkness, still scalding from the fire and brimstone of the depths. "Oi, oi, mana mou," "oi, oi, mana mou." And sometimes, less often, the sound of stifled breathing, like a snore, and those who knew said that was the rattle of death.

Sometimes they dragged along with them prisoners captured a few hours before in surprise raids by our patrols. Their breath stank of wine and their pockets were full of canned goods or chocolates. But we had nothing, the bridges cut off behind us and our few mules helpless in the snow and the slippery muck.

Finally the moment came when we saw smoke rising here and there in the distance, and along the horizon the first bright red flares.

b

THOUGH *very young I came to know the voices of a hundred years,*
Not the moment of piny creaking in the forest's heart,
Only the dog's howling on man-trodden mountains,
Smoke from low houses, and the other world's turmoil
In the unspeakable glance of those breathing their last.

Not the small stork cries dallying in the wind,
Or, when quiet falls like rain, the growling of vegetables,
Only the stifled and inarticulate writhing of animals,
The black circles under the Virgin's eyes, twice:
For the burial plain and the women's aprons.

Only the knocking at the door, and by the time you open: no one,
Not even the trace of a hand on the hair's light frost.
Though I've waited many years, quiet was never given me.
When sharing with my brothers, I was granted the shortened portion:
The pebble-studded harness and the serpent's ways.

RICHES you've never given me,
devastated as I've always been by the tribes of the Continents,
    also glorified by them always, arrogantly!
The North was granted the Vine
    and the South the Ear of Corn,
ransoming the wind's course,
    profanely cashing in
the trees' labor twice and thrice.
    I nothing,
knowing only heather in the sun's thorn,
    feeling only
a drop of water on my untrimmed beard
    while I laid my rough cheek on rougher stone
for ages and ages.
    I slept on the next day's worry
like a soldier on his rifle.
    I explored the night's bounties
like an ascetic his God.
    Out of my sweat they set a diamond
and stealthily supplanted
    the virgin of my eye.
They weighed my joy and said they found it wanting
    and they crushed it underfoot like an insect.
They crushed my joy underfoot and locked it in a stone
    and they finally left me with the stone,
my terrifying image.
    They pound it with a heavy axe, they pierce it with a hard drill,
they bruise it with a bitter chisel, my stone.
    And as time devours the substance, the oracle on my face
becomes clearer and clearer:

    FEAR THE WRATH OF THE DEAD
      AND THE STATUES OF THE ROCKS!

I ADDED UP my days yet did not find you
anywhere, ever, holding my hand
    in the roar of precipices and my confusion of stars!
Others took Knowledge and others Power,
    streaking darkness with effort,
fitting their withered faces
    with little masks of joy and sorrow.
Not I — I alone fit no masks
    but cast joy and sorrow behind me,
generously cast Power and Knowledge
    behind me.
I added up my days and was left alone.
    Others said: Why? He too should live
in a house with flower pots and a white bride.
    Horses, red and black, kindled in me
a stubborn urge for other, whiter Helens!
    I longed for another, more secret manliness,
and from where they hindered me, invisible, I galloped
    to return the rains to the fields
and to reclaim the blood of my unburied dead!
    Others said: Why? He too should know
life in the eyes of someone else.
    I did not see the eyes of anyone else but faced
only tears in the Void I was embracing,
    only thunderstorms in the quiet I was enduring.
I added up my days yet did not find you,
    and I took up my weapons and went out alone
in the roar of precipices and my confusion of stars!

ALONE *I governed my sorrow,*
Alone I colonized the abandoned month of May,
Alone I swelled fragrances
On fields in halcyon days,
Fed yellow to the flowers, herded the hills,
Shot red into the wilderness!
I said: the stab wound will not be deeper than the wounded cry,
And I said: Injustice will not be more venerable than blood!
The hand of earthquakes, the hand of famines,
The hand of foes and kin
Raged, destroyed, devastated, annihilated
Once and twice and three times over
Betrayed, I remained on the plain, alone,
Stormed, I was taken in the castle, alone,
The message I raised I endured alone!

Alone I discouraged death,
Alone I bit into Time with teeth of stone,
Alone I set off on the long journey
Like the trumpet's call through the skies.
Nemesis, steel and fraud were in my power,
I could have marched on with a cloud of dust and armaments.
I said: I'll compete with only the sword of cold waters,
And I said: I'll strike out with only the Stainless of my mind!
In spite of earthquakes, in spite of famines,
In spite of foes and kin,
I stood my ground, I held my own, I grew in spirit, grew in strength
Once and twice and three times over
I built my houses on memory, alone,
I took the halo and crowned myself, alone,
The wheat I heralded I reaped alone!

THE MULE DRIVERS

IN THOSE DAYS, at long last, after three full weeks, the first mule drivers reached our territory. And they told us a lot about the towns they'd passed through—Délvino, Saints Saránda, Koritsá. And they unloaded their salt herring and biscuits with an eye to finishing up as soon as possible and taking off. Because they weren't used to this booming from the mountains, it scared them, and so did the black beards on our wasted faces.

And it happened then that one of them had some old newspapers on him. And all of us read with amazement—though we'd heard rumors about it already—how they were celebrating in the capital and how people in the streets would carry on their shoulders those fighting men back on leave from their offices in Prevesa and Arta. And the bells would ring the day long, and in the evening at the theaters they would sing songs and act out our lives on stage for the crowd to applaud.

Heavy silence fell among us, because our souls had turned fierce from so many months in the wilderness, and, without saying so, we'd become very tight about what years we had left. In fact at one point Sergeant Zois, tears welling in his eyes, brushed aside the rags with news of the world, giving it the five-fingered sign. And the rest of us didn't say a thing, except that our eyes showed him something like gratitude.

Then Lefteris, who was standing off by himself rolling a cigarette stoically, as though carrying the helplessness of the universe on his shoulders, turned to say: "Sergeant, what's the point of fuming about it? Those who are ordained for herring and biscuits will always go back to herring and biscuits. And the same goes for those with their endless paperwork, and for those who make their soft beds but don't control them. But let me tell you one thing: only he who wrestles with the darkness inside him will find his own place in the sun someday." Then Zois: "So you think I don't have a wife and fields and troubles of my own, sitting here on watch in the wilderness?" And Lefteris answered: "The things one doesn't love, Sarge, are the things to fear, because they're lost already, no matter how much you try to cling to them. But there's no way you can lose the things of the heart, don't you worry, and that's what the wilderness works for. Sooner or later, those who

26

are meant to find them will find them." Then Zois asked again: "So who in your opinion is going to find them?" Then Lefteris, slowly, pointing his finger: "You and I, brother, and anybody else chosen by the moment that's listening to us."

And right then we heard, whistling dark in the air, the shell about to reach us. And we all hit the dirt and lay there face down on the brambles, because by now we knew the markings of the Invisible by heart, and our ears could spot in advance exactly where the fire would open the earth and spill out. And the fire didn't hurt a thing, only a few of the mules reared up on their hind legs and some others scattered in their fright. And as the smoke settled you could see the men who'd led them up there with so much trouble chasing after them with wild gestures. And their faces pale, they went on unloading the herring and biscuits with an eye to finishing up as soon as possible and taking off, because they weren't used to this booming from the mountains, it scared them, and so did the black beards on our wasted faces.

d

A SOLITARY SWALLOW *and a costly spring,*
For the sun to turn it takes a job of work,
It takes a thousand dead sweating at the Wheels,
It takes the living also giving up their blood.

God my Master Builder, You built me into the mountains,
God my Master Builder, You enclosed me in the sea!

Magicians carried off the body of May,
They buried the body in a tomb of the sea,
They sealed it up in a deep well,
Its scent fills the darkness and all the Abyss.

God my Master Builder, You too among the Easter lilacs,
God my Master Builder, You felt the scent of Resurrection!

Wriggling like sperm in a dark womb,
The terrible insect of memory breaks through the earth
And bites the light like a hungry spider,
Making the shores glow and the sea radiant.

God my Master Builder, You girded me with seashores,
God my Master Builder, You founded me on mountains.

V

My foundations on mountains,
and the people carry the mountains on their shoulders
and on these mountains memory burns
like the unconsumed bush.
Memory of my people, they call you Pindos and they call you Athos.
Time is in turmoil
and hangs days by the feet
emptying the bones of the humbled with a sudden clatter.
Who, how, when did they climb the abyss?
Which, whose, how many armies?
The face of the sky turns and my enemies have gone far away.
Memory of my people, they call you Pindos and they call you Athos.
You alone know the man by his heel,
You alone speak by the stone's cutting edge.
It is you who sharpens the features of the saints,
and you who drags the lilac of Resurrection
to the rim of the eternal waters!
You touch my mind and it hurts the infant of Spring!
You punish my hand and it turns whiter in the darkness!
You always pass through the fire to reach brightness.
You always pass through the brightness
to reach the top of snow-haloed mountains.
But what are the mountains? Who and what are on the mountains?
My foundations on mountains,
and the people carry the mountains on their shoulders
and on these mountains memory burns
like the unconsumed bush!

VI

THE POET of clouds and waves sleeps inside me!
His dark lips always on the hurricane's nipple
    and his soul always in the sea's kick
against the mountain's shin!
    The north wind invades from Thrace, uprooting oak trees.
Small craft rounding the cape
    suddenly turn over and vanish,
emerge again high among the clouds
    on the other side of the deep,
seaweed clinging to the anchors,
    to the beards of grieving saints.
Lovely rays around the face
    vibrate the halo of the open sea.
Old men fasting turn their vacant eyes that way,
    and the women clothe the immaculate whitewash
with their own black shadows.
    I too with them, moving my hand,
Poet of clouds and waves!
    Along with them I dip my brush
into the humble bucket and paint:
    the new hulls,
the gold and black icons!
    Saint Kanaris, be our aid and shelter!
Saint Miaoulis, be our aid and shelter!
    Saint Manto, be our aid and shelter!

VII

THEY CAME
dressed up as "friends,"
    came countless times, my enemies,
trampling the primeval soil.
    And the soil never blended with their heel.
They brought
    The Wise One, the Founder, and the Geometer,
Bibles of letters and numbers,
    every kind of Submission and Power,
to sway over the primeval light.
    And the light never blended with their roof.
Not even a bee was fooled into beginning the golden game,
    not even a Zephyr into swelling the white aprons.
On the peaks, in the valleys, in the ports
    they raised and founded
mighty towers and villas,
    floating timbers and other vessels;
and the Laws decreeing the pursuit of profit
    they applied to the primeval measure.
And the measure never blended with their thinking.
    Not even a footprint of a god left a mark on their soul,
not even a fairy's glance tried to rob them of their speech.
    They came
dressed up as "friends,"
    came countless times, my enemies,
bearing the primeval gifts.
    And their gifts were nothing else
but iron and fire only.
    To the open expecting fingers
only weapons and iron and fire.
    Only weapons and iron and fire.

VIII

THEY CAME
with their gold braid,
    the fowl of the North and the beasts of the East!
After dividing my flesh in two
    and quarreling finally over my liver,
they left.
    "Theirs the smoke of sacrifice," they said,
"and ours the smoke of fame,
    amen."
And the echo that was sent out of the past
    all of us heard and knew.
We knew the echo and once again
    we sang in a dry voice:
Ours, ours the bloody iron
    and the treble-wrought betrayal.
Ours the dawn light on bronze
    and teeth clenched until the final hour,
the bait and the invisible net.
    Ours to crawl on all fours,
ours the secret oath in the dark,
    the unfeeling glance,
and a never never Compensation.
    Brothers, they tricked us!
"Theirs the smoke of sacrifice," they said,
    "And ours the smoke of fame,
amen."
    But you, mouth of the innocent, gate of Paradise,
with your word you lit the star's lamp
    in our hand!
We see in the future the might of smoke,
    a plaything of your breath,
its power and its glory!

e

WITH THE STAR'S LAMP *I went out in the heavens.*
How, in the frost of the meadows, the world's only shore,
Can I find my soul, the four-leaf tear!

Weeping myrtle, silvered with sleep,
Sprinkled my face. I blow and go alone.
How can I find my soul, the four-leaf tear!

Leader of rays and magus of bedrooms,
Vagabond who knows the future, speak to me.
How can I find my soul, the four-leaf tear!

My girls are in mourning for the ages,
My boys carry guns yet do not know
How I can find my soul, the four-leaf tear!

Nights with a hundred hands stir my entrails
Throughout the firmament. This pain burns.
How can I find my soul, the four-leaf tear!

With the star's lamp I roam the heavens.
In the frost of the meadows, the world's only shore,
How can I find my soul, the four-leaf tear!

THE GREAT SALLY

IN THOSE DAYS the boys organized a secret meeting and decided, because the news in the capital was getting worse and worse, to move out into the streets and squares with the only thing they had left: a handful of territory under their open shirts, with its black hair and the sun's tiny cross — there where the Spring has power and sway.

And since it was close to the day when the Nation used to celebrate the other Rising, they chose that day again for the Sally. And they came out early in full view of the sun, with fearlessness spread from top to bottom like a flag, the young men with swollen feet, those they called bums. And many men followed, many women, and the wounded with their bandages and crutches. And suddenly you'd see their faces so lined that you'd think many days had gone by in those few hours.

And the Others, hearing about such daring impudence, were greatly disturbed. And after sizing up their own possessions three times over, they decided to move out into the streets and squares with the only thing they had left: a yard of fire under their steel, with the black muzzles and the sun's teeth — there where no sprig or blossom ever shed a tear. And they hit at random, their eyes shut out of desperation. And Spring overran them more and more. As though there were no other road in the whole world for Spring to take except this one, and as though they themselves had taken it silently, gazing far ahead, beyond the edge of despair, at the Serenity they were destined to become — these young men with swollen feet, those they called bums, and the men and the women, and the wounded with their bandages and crutches.

And many days went by in those few hours. And the beasts cut down a multitude and rounded up others. And the following day they lined up thirty against the wall.

f

INTELLIGIBLE *sun of Justice and you, glorifying myrtle,*
do not, I implore you, do not forget my country!

Its high mountains eagle-shaped, its volcanos all vines in rows,
and its houses the whiter for neighboring near the blue!

Though touching Asia on one side and Europe a little on the other,
it stands there alone in the air and alone in the sea!

Neither a foreigner's concept nor a kinsman's one love,
but mourning, oh, everywhere and the relentless light!

My bitter hands circle with the Thunderbolt to the other side of Time,
I summon my old friends with threats and running blood!

But the blood has all been ransomed and, oh, the threats quarried,
and the winds rush in now, the one against the other!

Intelligible sun of Justice and you, glorifying myrtle,
do not, I implore you, do not forget my country!

THIS is he,
our own ever invisible Judas!
    Seven portals cover him,
seven armies grow fat in his diocese.
    Aerial machines carry him off,
heavy with fur and tortoise shell,
    to deposit him inside the Elysées and the White Houses.
And no language is his own, because all are his —
    And no woman is his own, because all are his —
the Almighty!
    The naive look on him in wonder,
and close to the gleam of crystal the dark-suited men smile,
    and the half-naked tigresses
leap up in the lairs of Lycabettus!
    And no passage open for the sun to carry his fame into the future,
and no Day of Judgment, because
    we, brothers, we are the Day of Judgment
and ours the hand that will be immortalized —
    casting the silver pieces in his face!

X

THEY MOCKED ME to my face, the young Alexandrians:
"Look," they said, "the naive tourist of the century—
    so insensitive:
when the rest of us mourn, he rejoices,
    and again, when the rest of us rejoice,
he turns glum for no reason.
    Indifferent, he walks past our cries,
and with his ear to the stone,
    alone and earnest,
he notices things invisible to us.
    A man with no friend
or follower,
    who trusts his body only
and looks for the great mystery inside the sun's thorny leaves,
    this is he,
the outcast of the century's marketplaces!
    Because he has no mind
and makes no profit out of the tears of others,
    and on the bush that burns our anguish
he only condescends to piss.
    The antichrist and callous satanist of the century!
When the rest of us mourn,
    he wears the sun.
And when the rest of us taunt,
    he wears ideas.
And when the rest of us announce peace,
    he wears a knife."
So they mocked me to my face, the young Alexandrians!

g

THIS *world this world is one and the same world*
Of suns and dust, of turmoil and quiet evenings,
Weaver of constellations, silver-gilder of moss,
At the waning of memory and the exit of dreams,
This world, this same world is both
A cymbal, a cymbal, and vain distant laughter!

This world this world is one and the same world,
Carrion of sensuality, rapist of fountains,
Soaring above Floods, plunging under Typhoons,
Clawed, hunched, shaggy, red-haired,
By night with the syrinx, by day with the lyre,
On the cobblestones of cities, the jib-sails of meadows,
Flat-headed, long-headed,
Willing, unwilling,
Both Solomon and the son of Haggith.

This world this world is one and the same world
Of ebbing and orgasm, of remorse and clouding,
Inventor of zodiacs, daredevil of domes
At the rim of the ecliptic, at the farthest reach of Creation,
This world, this same world is both
Brass, sounding brass, and a vain distant cloud!

THE VACANT LOT WITH THE NETTLES

ONE OF THE SUNLESS days of that winter, on a Saturday morning, lots of cars and motorcycles surrounded Lefteris's neighborhood, with its tin shutters full of holes and its sewer ditches along the street. And shouting wildly, from those cars and motorcycles came men with faces cast in lead and straight hair like straw. They ordered all the men to gather in the vacant lot full of nettles. And they were armed from head to toe, their muzzles leveled at the crowd. And the boys were really scared, because as it happened, almost all of them had some secret hidden in their pocket or their soul. But there was no way out. So making duty out of necessity, they lined up, and the men with leaden faces, straw hair, and black boots fenced them in with barbed wire. And they cut the clouds in two and sleet came down so hard that jaws could hardly keep their teeth in place.

Then, from the far side, walking slowly, the Man with the Hood appeared, his finger ready to point, and the hours shuddered on the great clock of angels. And whoever he chose to stand in front of was hauled out by the hair and thrown to the ground to be trampled. Until the moment came when he stood in front of Lefteris. But Lefteris didn't budge. He only raised his eyes slowly and gazed so far away — far into his own future — that the other felt the jolt and tilted back, almost falling. And rabid, he nearly raised his black hood to spit in his face. But again Lefteris didn't budge.

At that moment, the Great Foreigner with three stripes on his collar, following along behind, put his hands on his hips and snarled: "Look," he said. "Look at the men who say they want to change the course of the world!" And the miserable man, not knowing what truth he'd spoken, lashed his whip three times across Lefteris's face. And for the third time Lefteris didn't budge. Then, blinded by the worthless power in his hands, the Foreigner, not knowing what he was doing, drew his revolver and blasted it at the root of Lefteris's right ear.

And the boys were very frightened; and the men with leaden faces, straw hair, and black boots turned waxen. Because the shacks all around shook as in an earthquake, and in many places the tarpaper fell off the walls, and far off, behind the sun, women appeared weeping, kneeling down in a vacant lot full of nettles and black clotted blood. While the great clock of angels chimed exactly twelve.

h

I TURNED *my eyes full of tears*
toward the window.
And gazing out at the snow-whitened
trees of the valley,
I said: "Brothers, even these
they'll defile one day.
The hooded men, in the century ahead,
are getting their nooses ready."

I bit into the day: not a single drop
of green blood dripped.
I shouted at the gates: my voice took on
the grief of murderers.
In the earth's center appeared the nucleus
growing darker and darker
And the sun's ray, look, became
the guiding thread of Death!

Oh bitter women dressed in black,
virgins and mothers,
You who gave water at the fountain
to the angels' nightingales,
Even you were given, by Charon himself,
your handful of fate.
Out of the wells you now draw cries
of those unjustly killed.

Fire and rancor so fail to mingle
that my people must starve.
God's wheat was loaded and hauled away
on their giant trucks.
In the desolate and empty city
only the hand remains
To paint across the great walls
BREAD AND FREEDOM.

Night blew, the houses went out,
and it's late inside my soul.
No one hears me wherever I knock,
memory kills me.
It says: "Brothers, black hours are near,
time will tell.
The joys of men have soiled
the guts of monsters."

I turned my eyes full of tears
toward the window,
I shouted at the gates: my voice took on
the grief of murderers.
In the earth's center appeared the nucleus
growing darker and darker
And the sun's ray, look, became
the guiding thread of Death!

BROTHERS, I shout, wherever you are,
wherever your foot may tread,
   build a fountain,
your own Mavroyeni fountain.
   The water good,
and the hand of noon all stone,
   holding the sun in its open palm.
The flow is cool, I will rejoice.
   Let speech that knows no lie
recite my mind out loud,
   let my guts become clearly legible.
I can't go on,
   the gallows have annihilated my trees
and my eyes turn black.
   I can't endure,
even the crossroads I knew have turned into dead ends.
   Mace-wielding Seljuks lie in wait.
Vulture-headed Chagans plot in the dark.
   Dog-fuckers and corpse-eaters and gloom-addicts
rule the future with excrement.
   Brothers, wherever evil finds you,
wherever your minds grow muddled,
   invoke Dionysios Solomos,
invoke Alexandros Papadiamandis.
   Speech that knows no lie
will put to rest the face of martyrdom
   with some tint of azure on the lips.
The water good,
   and the hand of noon all stone,
holding the sun in its open palm.
   Wherever your foot may tread, I shout,
build, brothers, ·
   build a fountain,
your own Mavroyeni fountain!

XII

AND in the heart of midnight, in the rice fields of sleep,
lack of wind tortures me, and the Moon's evil mosquito!
    I wrestle with the sheets, and with my eyes thick,
I vainly try out the darkness:
    Winds — bearded old men —
guardians and key-bearers of my ancient seas,
    you who hold the secret,
draw a dolphin before my eyes,
    before my eyes draw a dolphin,
make it swift, and Greek, and make the hour eleven!
    Let it cross and rub out the altar's tablet
and change the meaning of martyrdom.
    Let its white surf surge
to drown the Bird of Prey and the Priest!
    Let it cross and loosen the shape of the Cross
and give its wood back to the tree.
    Let the deep creaking remind me still
that he who I am exists!
    Let its broad tail furrow my memory
out of an unplotted path
    and leave me in the sun once again
like an ancient pebble of the Cyclades!
    I wrestle with the sheets, and with my hands blind,
I vainly try out the darkness:
    Winds — bearded old men —
guardians and key-bearers of my ancient seas,
    you who hold the secret,
strike the Trident into my heart
    and cross it with the dolphin,
the sign which I myself truly am,
    that I may ascend with my first youth
to the azure of the sky — and there have dominion!

43

XIII

INIQUITIES have stained my hands, how can I open them?
Armed guards have filled my eyes, where can I look?
      Sons of men, what can I say?
Earth bears the horrible and the soul the twice horrible!
      Good for you, my first youth and untamed lip,
you who taught the storm's pebble
      and in the midst of squalls talked back to the thunder,
Good for you, my first youth!
      You threw so much earth on my roots that even my thought turned green!
So much light in my blood that even my love
      took on the sky's power and meaning.
I'm clean from end to end
      and in the hands of Death a useless vessel,
bad prey in the claws of the brutal.
      Sons of men, what am I to fear?
Take away my entrails, I have sung!
      Take away my sea with its white north winds,
the wide window full of lemon trees,
      the many bird songs, and the one girl
whose joy when I merely touched her was enough for me,
      take them away, I have sung!
Take away my dreams, how can you read them?
      Take away my thoughts, where will you utter them?
I am clean from end to end.
      Kissing, I enjoyed the virgin body.
Blowing, I colored the fleece of the sea.
      All my ideas I turned into islands.
I squeezed lemon on my conscience.

XIV

TEMPLES in the shape of the sky
and beautiful girls
	with grapes between the teeth — you were right for us!
Birds nullifying on high the weight of our hearts
	and so much blue we have loved!
Gone, gone,
	July with its lucent shirt
and stony August with its small, uneven stairs.
	Gone.
And in the eyes of the depths the starfish remained untranslated,
	and in the depths of the eyes the sunset remained undelivered!
And the prudence of men closed the borders;
	walled up the sides of the world,
raised the nine bastions skywards,
	slaughtered the body on the altar's slab,
and posted many guards at the exits.
	So the prudence of men closed the borders.
Temples in the shape of the sky
	and beautiful girls
with grapes between the teeth — you were right for us!
	Birds nullifying on high the weight of our hearts
and so much blue we have loved!
	Gone, gone,
Maistros with his pointed sandal
	and thoughtless Graigos with his slanting red sails.
Gone,
	and deep under the soil clouds gathered,
raising black gravel
	and thunderclaps, the wrath of the dead;
and slowly, creaking in the wind,
	their chests thrust out, terrifying,
the statues of the rocks returned again!

LEAVING *the clouds behind them,*
The statues of the rocks go voyaging,
Chest forward, as though to thrust
Into the wind things to come
So the vultures won't smell out these too and swoop down!

With the church bell chiming death
The village flocks came down
To the slopes overlooking the sea
And a voice agitated the winds:
"Boys, hunger has darkened our soul!"

The secret factories of nations
Forge metal out of wheat,
Feeding the monster they do not want,
And its mouth grows gigantic
Until nobody is left—only creaking bones!

But first, in the valley that quaked,
As if moaning Hades had howled,
The roofs of the houses came unnailed
To reveal—unhoped-for miracle—
Women listening silently to the wailing of their infants!

Life that has tasted death
Returned naked like the sun,
And with nothing else left,
Life that squandered everything
Nailed upon the ruins, oh, a single radiant poppy!

If the vulture ever gave back
The voice of the lamb it has gored,
With our ear to the grass we might hear
The wrath of the dead training
To snatch the darkness with one hand and reveal itself with the other!

THE COURTYARD OF LAMBS

MY PEOPLE said: "The justice I was taught I practiced, and look, for centuries I've grown tired waiting naked outside the closed gateway to the courtyard of lambs. The flock knew my voice, and it leapt up and bleated at my every whistle. But others, often the very ones who praised my endurance, jumping down from trees or walls, were the first to set foot in the middle of the courtyard of lambs. And there I was, always naked, with no flock" — so moaned my people. And on their teeth ancient hunger gleamed, and their soul creaked in its bitterness as the boot of the desperate man creaks on gravel.

Then those who own a great deal, when they heard this creaking, were frightened. Because they know how to read every sign in detail, and often, from miles away, they can make out what profits them. So right away they put on the sandals of treachery. And half of them on one side and half on the other, they pulled the rest to and fro, saying: "Your deeds are good and fine, and here you see the closed gateway to the courtyard of lambs. Raise your hand and we are with you, and we'll take care of the fire and the iron. Don't worry about homes, don't feel sorry for families, don't ever let the voice of son or father or younger brother stop you. Should any one of you worry or feel sorry or stop, let him know this: his will be the sin, and on his head will fall the fire and iron we brought."

And before they had finished speaking, the weather had begun to change far away in the blackness of the clouds and nearby in the human flock. And it seemed the wind had come by low, moaning, and had thrown the bodies aside empty, without a drop of memory. Their faces blue and mute, turned upwards, but their hands deep in the pocket, clutching a piece of iron — a fire rod or one of those with a sharp tip and a honed edge. And they marched, one against the other, the one not knowing the other. And the son took aim against the father, and the older brother against the younger. So that many homes were left undone, and many women had to wear black two and three times in a row. And when you tried to go out a little farther, nothing. Only the wind wailing through the beams. And here and there, on the few charred rocks, smoke feeding on the remains of the slain.

Thirty-three months and more the Evil lasted. While they kept on

47

knocking at the gate of lambs. And no lamb's voice was heard except under the knife. Nor the gate's voice, except at the hour when it sank into the final flames to burn. Because my people are the gate and the gateway and the flock of lambs.

j

THE BLOOD *of love has robed me in purple*
And joys never seen before have covered me in shade.
I've become corroded in the south wind of humankind
Mother far away, my Everlasting Rose.

On the open sea they lay in wait for me,
With triple-masted men-of-war they bombarded me,
My sin that I too had a love of my own
Mother far away, my Everlasting Rose.

Once in July her large eyes
Half-opened, deep down my entrails, to light up
The virgin life for a single moment
Mother far away, my Everlasting Rose.

And since that day the wrath of ages
Has turned on me, shouting out the curse:
"He who saw you, let him live in blood and stone"
Mother far away, my Everlasting Rose.

Once again I took the shape of my native country,
I grew and flowered among the stones.
And the blood of killers I redeem with light
Mother far away, my Everlasting Rose.

XV

I WAS YOUR WILL, my God, and here I pay you back.
I did not grant forgiveness,
     I did not give in to supplication,
I endured the desert like a pebble.
     What else, what else lies ahead for me?
I lead the flock of stars into your arms,
     and Dawn, before I can stop her,
has lured them far away into her nets,
     and she is your will!
Hills with castles and fruit-bearing seas
     I prop up against the wind
and the church bell of twilight slowly drinks them in,
     and that bell is your will!
I raise grass as though shouting with all my senses
     and there it is drooping again,
scorched by the heat of July,
     and this heat is your will!
What else then, what else new, lies ahead for me?
     Look, it is you who speak and I who come true,
I hurl the stone and it lands on me.
     I deepen mines and elaborate the skies.
I hunt the birds and lose myself in their weight.
     I was your will, my God, and here I pay you back.
The elements that you are,
     days and nights,
suns and stars, storms and serenity,
     I subvert into order and set against
my own death,
     which is also your will!

XVI

I ROUSED the sensual pleasures early,
lit my poplar early,
    arm thrust out I moved ahead to the sea
and there, alone, I set it up:
    You blew and storms surrounded me,
one by one you took away my birds—
    My God, you were calling me, how was I to escape?
I looked into the future at the months and years
    that will come back again without me
and bit myself so deeply
    that I felt my blood slowly rise
and drip out of my future.
    I dug in the earth at the hour of my guilt
and trembling I lifted the victim in my arms
    and spoke to it so gently
that its eyes slowly opened and dripped dew
    on the earth where I stood in my guilt:
I flung the darkness on the bed of love
    with worldly things naked in my mind,
and I shot my sperm so far
    that women turned slowly under the sun, in pain,
and once again gave birth to the visible.
    My God, you were calling me, how was I to escape?
I roused the sensual pleasures early,
    lit my poplar early,
arm thrust out I moved ahead to the sea
    and there, alone, I set it up:
You blew and my entrails yearned,
    one by one the birds came back to me!

k

I WILL TONSURE *my head, monk of things verdant,*
And reverently serve the order of birds,
I will come to the matins of Fig Trees out of the night,
Dew-covered, to bring in my apron
Blue, pink, purple
And to kindle the generous water drops,
I the more generous.

I will have for icons the immaculate girls
Dressed only in the linen of the open sea,
I will pray that my purity assume
The myrtle's instinct and the muscle of wild animals,
To drown forever in my vigorous entrails
The mean, the perverse, the nebulous,
I the more vigorous.

There will be times of much iniquity,
Of profit and honor, of remorse and flogging,
The maddened Bucephalus of blood will charge
To trample my white yearning,
Valor, love, light,
And smelling them out as mighty, to neigh,
He the more mighty.

But then, at the sixth hour of the erect lilies,
When my judgment will make a crack in Time,
The eleventh Commandment will emerge from my eyes:
Either this world or none other shall be
The Labor of Birth, the Union with God, the Forever,
Which in the justice of my soul I will have proclaimed,
I the more just.

PROPHETIC

MANY YEARS after Sin – which they called Virtue in the churches and gave it their blessing – and after the storm – which will be given birth by the mind of man – will have swept relics of old stars and cobwebbed corners of the heavens, then Creation, paying for the works of ancient Rulers, shall shudder. Turmoil will fall upon Hades, and the planking will sag under the sun's great pressure. But first the sun will withhold its rays, a sign that the time has come for dreams to take their revenge. And then the sun will speak, saying: "Exiled Poet, speak, in your century what do you see?"

—— I see the nations, once arrogant, abandoned to the wasp and the wood sorrel.

—— I see axes in the air splitting the busts of Emperors and Generals.

—— I see merchants stooping to cash in the dividends of their own cadavers.

—— I see the coherence of secret meanings.

Many years after Sin – which they called Virtue in the churches and gave it their blessing: but before this, behold, there will be the beautiful "Philips" and "Roberts," narcissistic at the crossroads. They will wear their rings reversed, comb their hair with an iron nail, adorn their chests with skulls to lure the fancy women. And the fancy women will be amazed and acquiesce. So that the word may come true that the day is at hand when beauty will be surrendered to the flies of the Marketplace. And the whore's body will be outraged, having nothing else to envy. And the whore will turn plaintiff against the wise and the great, bringing as witness the seed she has faithfully served. And she will shake off the curse, stretching her arm toward the East, and shout: "Exiled Poet, speak, in your century what do you see?"

—— I see the colors of Hymmetus at the holy base of our New Civil Code.

—— I see young Myrto, the whore from Sikinos, a stone statue unveiled in the Marketplace of the Fountains and the standing Lions.

—— I see the boys and the girls at the annual Lottery of Couples.

—— I see, high in the air, the Erechtheum of Birds.

After the storm – which was given birth by the mind of man – will have swept relics of old stars and cobwebbed corners of the heavens: but before this, behold, generations will pass their plow over the barren earth. And secretly the Rulers will count their human merchandise, declaring wars; there the Policeman and the Military Judge will have their fill, leaving the gold to the obscure so that they collect the wages of hubris and martyrdom. And great ships will spread their flags, marching songs will conquer the streets, balconies will shower the Victor with flowers, while he will live in the stench of corpses. And darkness will open to his measure the mouth of the grave near him, shouting: "Exiled Poet, speak, in your century what do you see?"

——I see the Military Judges burning like candles at the great banquet of the Resurrection.

——I see the Police offering their blood as a sacrifice to the cleanliness of the skies.

——I see the perpetual revolution of plants and flowers.

—— I see the gunboats of Love.

Then Creation, paying for the works of ancient Rulers, shall shudder. Turmoil will fall upon Hades, and the planking will sag under the sun's great pressure. But before this, behold, the young will sigh and their blood grow old for no reason. Cropped convicts will rattle their mess cans against the iron bars. And all the factories will empty, only to fill up again under requisition, so that they can produce preserved dreams in myriad boxes and a thousand brands of bottled nature. And years will come, pale and weak in their bandages. And everybody will have his few ounces of happiness. And the things inside him will already be beautiful ruins. Then the Poet, having no other place of exile in which to lament, emptying the storm's health from his open chest, will return to stand among the beautiful ruins inside. And then the last of men will say his first word: that the grass shall grow tall and that woman shall rise at his side like a sun's ray. And again he will worship the woman and lay her upon the grass, as was ordained. And dreams will take their revenge, and they will sow generations forever and ever!

1

I OPEN *my mouth and the sea rejoices*
And carries my words to its dark caves
And whispers them gently to the little seals
That weep in the night over the troubles of men.

I carve my veins and the dreams turn red
To become hoops in the children's alleys
And sheets for the girls lying awake
Secretly listening to the marvels of love.

Dizzy with honeysuckle I go down to my garden
And bury the bodies of my secret dead,
Cut the golden cord of their betrayed stars
So they can fall free into the abyss.

The iron turns rusty and I punish its century,
I who suffered the myriad piercing points,
Out of violets and hyacinths I fashion
A new knife fit for Heroes.

I bare my breast and the winds are unleashed,
They sweep away ruins and broken souls,
And clear the earth of its murky clouds
So to reveal the Meadows of Bliss!

XVII

I'M ON my way now to a far and sinless country.
Now I'm followed by airy creatures
  with polar iridescence in their hair,
and gentle gilding on their skin.
  I sail through the grass with my knee for a prow,
and my breath clears from the face of the earth
  the last clusters of sleep.
And the trees walk by my side against the wind.
  I see mysteries great and strange:
Helen's crypt a crystal fountain.
  The sign of the Cross a Trident wound by a dolphin.
The unholy barbed wire a white gateway
  through which I will pass in glory.
The words that betrayed me, the insulting blows,
  having become myrtle and branches of palm
meaning: Hosanna to the coming one!
  I see destitution as the pleasure of fruit,
slanting olive groves with blue between the fingers,
  the years of wrath now behind iron bars.
And the depths of Marina an immense shore
  moistened by the sorcery of beautiful eyes,
where I in my purity will walk.
  The tears that betrayed me and the humiliations
having become breaths and never-setting birds
  meaning: Hosanna to the coming one!
I'm on my way now to a far and sinless country.

XVIII

I'M ON my way now to a far and unwrinkled country.
Now I'm followed by dark blue girls
    and small stone horses
with the sun's tiny wheel on their wide brows.
    Generations of myrtle have recognized me
ever since I trembled on the water's sacred screen
    crying holy, holy.
He, the conqueror of Hades and the savior of Eros,
    he is Prince of Lilies.
And I saw myself painted for a moment
    by those same Cretan breaths.
So that the crocus might be vindicated by the skies.
    Now to lime I entrust
My true Laws.
    Blessed, I say, are the potent ones who decipher the Undefiled.
For their teeth the intoxicating nipple
    on the breast of volcanoes and the vines of virgins.
Let them follow in my steps!
    I'm on my way to a far and unwrinkled country.
Now it is the hand of Death
    that grants the gift of Life
and sleep does not exist.
    The noon bell chimes
and slowly on the scorching stones letters are carved:
    NOW and FOREVER and PRAISED BE.
Forever forever and now and now the birds sing
    PRAISED BE the price paid.

THE GLORIA

PRAISED BE the light and man's

first rock-carved prayer

the vigor in the beast leading the sun

the plant that warbled so the day rose

The land that dives and rears its back

a stone horse the sea rides

the myriad tiny blue voices

the great white head of Poseidon

PRAISED BE the Mermaid's hand

holding the schooner as though to save it

as though to dedicate it to the winds

as though to drop it yet not really

The small heron on top of the church

nine in the morning like fragrant bergamot

a pure pebble down in the depths

the roofs and plantations of the azure sky

THE TOLLING WINDS that perform liturgies

that raise the sea like the Holy Virgin

that blow and set the oranges on fire

that whistle for the mountains and they come running

Beardless midshipmen of the storming sea

runners who've covered celestial miles

    those Hermae with their pointed hats

and the black smoke's heralding wand

    Maistros, Levantes, Garbis

    Pounentes, Graigos, Siroccos

    Ostria, Tramountana

PRAISED BE the wooden table

the blond wine with the sun's stain

    the water doodling across the ceiling

the philodendron on duty in the corner

The walls hand in hand with the waves

a foot that gathered wisdom in the sand

    a cicada that convinced a thousand others

conscience radiant like a summer

PRAISED BE the heatwave hatching

the beautiful boulders under the bridge

    the shit of children with its green flies

a sea boiling and no end to it

The sixteen deck hands hauling the net

the restless sea gull slowly cruising

    stray voices out of the wilderness

a shadow's crossing through the wall

THE ISLANDS with all their minium and lampblack

the islands with the vertebra of some Zeus

    the islands with their boat yards so deserted

the islands with their drinkable blue volcanoes

Facing the meltemi with jib close-hauled

Riding the southwester on a reach

    the full length of them covered with foam

with dark blue pebbles and heliotropes

Sifnos, Amorgos, Alonnisos

Thasos, Ithaka, Santorini

Kos, Ios, Sikinos

PRAISED BE Myrto standing

on the stone parapet facing the sea

    like a beautiful eight or a clay pitcher

holding a straw hat in her hand

The white and porous middle of day

the down of sleep lightly ascending

    the faded gold inside the arcades

and the red horse breaking free

    Hera of the tree's ancient trunk

the vast laurel grove, the light-devouring

    a house like an anchor down in the depths

and Kyra-Penelope twisting her spindle

    The straits for birds from the opposite shore

a citron from which the sky spilled out

    the blue hearing half under the sea

the long-shadowed whispering of nymphs and maples

    PRAISED BE, on the remembrance day

of the holy martyrs Cyricus and Julitta,

    a miracle burning threshing floors in the heavens

priests and birds chanting the *Ave:*

    HAIL Girl Burning and hail Girl Verdant

Hail Girl Unrepenting, with the prow's sword

    Hail you who walk and the footprints vanish

Hail you who wake and the miracles are born

Hail O Wild One of the depths' paradise

Hail O Holy One of the islands' wilderness

Hail Mother of Dreams, Girl of the Open Seas

Hail O Anchor-bearer, Girl of the Five Stars

Hail you of the flowing hair, gilding the wind

Hail you of the lovely voice, tamer of demons

Hail you who ordain the Monthly Ritual of the Gardens

Hail you who fasten the Serpent's belt of stars

Hail O Girl of the just and modest sword

Hail O Girl prophetic and daedalic

PRAISED BE the soil that raises

a smell of thunder as though from sulphur

    the floor of mountains where the dead

blossom as the flowers of tomorrow

    The never hesitating law of instinct

the pulse, life's fast player

    the clot of blood that is the sun's twin

and the ivy, high jumper of winters

    PRAISED BE the scarab-shaped knocker

the brash tooth in icy sunshine

    April sensing the change of sex

in the fountain's bud just as it opens

    The wheelbarrow tilting on its side

the goldbug that set fire to the future

    the water's invisible aorta throbbing

to make the gardenia stay alive

    THE HOME-FED FLOWERS of Nostalgia

the trembling flowers, infants of rain

    the small and four-legged ones on the footpath

those high among suns, and the dream-walking

The modest with red engagement rings

the haughty riding across the meadows

those fashioned of pure sky

the thoughtful, and those inlaid with chimeras

Lily, Rose, Jasmine

Violet, Lilac, Hyacinth

Carnation, Narcissus, Aster

PRAISED BE the cloud on the grass

the swoosh of a lizard on a wet ankle

Mnisareti's deep gaze

not the lamb's yet granting forgiveness

The bell's gold-evoking wind

the rider westbound to his ascension

and that other unseen rider heading

to impale the coming hour of decay

The windless calm of a night in June

jasmine and petticoats in the garden

the pet animal of the stars climbing

the moment of joy just before tears

67

A drop of soul and no word said

Aretousa like an empty window

    and love "descending from the heavens

having donned a purple tunic."

    THE GIRLS, blue grass of utopia

the girls, those Pleiades led astray

    the girls, those Vessels of the Mysteries

full to the brim yet bottomless

    Astringent in the dark yet marvelous

carved out in light yet all darkness

    turning on themselves like a lighthouse

the sun-devouring, the moon-walking

        Ersi, Myrto, Marina

       Eleni, Roxani, Fotini

          Anna, Alexandra, Cynthia

    The hatching of whispers inside seashells

one lost like a dream: Arignota

    a distant light that says: sleep

bewildered kisses like a crowd of trees

The bit of blouse the wind eats

the mossy peach fuzz on the shin

    the cunt's violet-scented salt

and the cold water of the Full Moon

PRAISED BE the distant song

Eleni's innermost bay with its ripple

    the barbary figs shining in the armpits

ruined sites of the future and the spider

The endless night-shifts in the entrails

the sleepless clock that's no good at all

    a black bed that keeps on floating

along the Galaxy's rugged shores

THE SHIPS upright on black feet

the ships, those goats of the Hyperboreans

    the ships, pawns of the North Star and Sleep

the ships, those Evadnes and Nicothoas

Full of gales and the hazels of Athos

smelling of dregs and ancient carobs

    their bows painted like the icons of saints

heeling and motionless all at once

Angelica, Polar, the Three Fathers

the Intrepid, the Halcyon, the Sea Lord

Maraki, In God We Trust, the Annunciation

PRAISED BE the wave growing wild

rising five fathoms high

the hair spilled to the vulture turning

to strike the windowpanes in a storm

Marina as she was before she existed

with the wild dog's skull and the demons

Marina, the moon's crescent horn

Marina, the world's doom and destruction

The quays open to the southern gale

the priest of the clouds who changes his mind

those poor little houses one on the other

leaning gently and falling asleep

the sad face of the passing rain

the virgin olive tree climbing the hill

no voice in the tired clouds

the small town's snail that was crushed

70

PRAISED BE you the bitter one

the lonely one, lost from the start

Poet practicing with a knife

in his third hand, the indelible one:

FOR HE is Death and he Life

He the Unforeseen and he the Laws

He the plant's straight line cutting across the body

He the focus of the lens burning the spirit

He the thirst that comes after the fountain

He the war that comes after the peace

He the watcher of waves, the Ion

He the Pygmalion of fires and monsters

He the fuse that lips ignite

He the unseen tunnel that outflanks Hades

He sensuality's Thief who can't be crucified

He the Serpent who unites with the Ear of Corn

He the darkness and he the beautiful folly

He the vernal essence of the showers of light

71

PRAISED BE the wolf's snout

changing to man's and his to an angel's

the nine steps that Plotinus climbed

the earthquake's chasm that filled with flowers

The slightest touch left by the sea gull

lighting up the pebbles like innocence

the line scarred upon your soul

signaling the grief of Paradise

PRAISED BE the underworld trumpeting

and the fiery yellow before the vision

the burning poem, death's echoing chamber

the spear-tipped and suicidal words

The inward light dawning pearl

in the image and likeness of the infinite

uncasted mountains turning out

identical images of eternity

THE MOUNTAINS arrogant like ancient ruins

the mountains heavy and sullen mammals

the mountains like a vision's submerged reefs,

closed in everywhere yet with forty passes

Those filled with drizzle like the monasteries

tucked away in the mist of sheep

those walking calmly like herdsmen

wearing the black vest and the headscarf

Pindus, Rodopi, Parnassus

Olympus, Tymphristos, Taygetus

Dirfys, Athos, Ainos

PRAISED BE the mountain saddle that opens

an eternally blue road in clouds

a voice mislaid deep in the valley

an echo drunk by the day like balsam

The effort of oxen dragging westward

the heavy groves of olive trees

the smoke unruffled on its way

to find and dissolve the works of man

PRAISED BE the oil lamp's motion

black with shadows and full of ruins

the page written under the soil

the song Liyeri sang in Hades

73

The monsters carved on the icon screen

the ancient poplars, bearers of fish

the lovable Korae of the stone arm

Helen's neck so like a shoreline

THE TREES starry with good will

the musical notation of another world

the ancient belief that there always exists

the very near yet still unseen

The shadow that bends them against the earth

something yellow in their remembering

their ancient dancing over graves

their wisdom that has no price to it

Olive, Pomegranate, Peach

Pine, Poplar, Plane Tree

Oak, Beech, Cypress

PRAISED BE the unmotivated tear

rising slowly in the lovely eyes

of children standing hand in hand

of children staring speechlessly

74

Love's stammering upon the rocks

a lighthouse discharging the grief of ages

  a cricket insisting like remorse

a woolen sweater left to the frost

  Perjured mint astringent to the teeth

lips that couldn't yield — and yet

  the "good-by" shining briefly on the lashes

then the eternally turbid world

  The storms' slow and heavy organ

Heraclitus in his ruined voice

  the other, the invisible side of killers

the tiny "why" that remained unanswered

  PRAISED BE the hand returning

from terrible murder knowing now

  which the world that is really superior

which the world's "now," which its "forever":

  Now the myrtle's wild animal   Now the cry of May

FOREVER the utmost conscience   Forever the full light

  Now now the hallucination and the mimicry of sleep

Forever forever the word and forever the astral Keel

75

Now the moving cloud of lepidoptera

Forever the circumgyrating light of mysteries

Now the crust of the Earth and the Dominion

Forever the food of the Soul and the quintessence

Now the Moon's incurable swarthiness

Forever the Galaxy's golden blue scintillation

Now the amalgam of peoples and the black Number

Forever the statue of Justice and the great Eye

Now the humiliation of the Gods   Now the ashes of Man

Now Now the zero

and Forever this small world the Great!

NOTES

NOTES

In the Greek Orthodox ecclesiastical tradition, these two words (meaning "worthy it is") have a double Mariolatric connotation: first, the title of a Byzantine hymn glorifying the Virgin Mother of God; and second, the name of a famous holy icon of the Virgin still extant on Mount Athos.

"The Genesis"

The form of this section consists of seven "paragraphs" or "hymns" written in free verse, with a refrain at the end. According to the poet's commentary (see the Preface, p. xiii), each "paragraph" corresponds to a stage of the Creation, of the Ages of Man, of the hours from dawn to midday (the section ends with nighttime, because the day's progress is abruptly interrupted by the appearance of Danger, incarnated by the Others and coinciding with the poet's maturity).

P. 3, l. 13
the three Black Women: The three Fates who preside over man's birth in both the ancient and the modern Greek traditions.

P. 3, l. 33
the Seven Axes: The name of the neighborhood in Herakleion (Crete) where the poet was born. The name derives from the axes that symbolize the seven Turkish regiments which conquered the city in 1669. Shortly after the poet's birth (in 1912), Crete was united with Greece, and these axes were taken down from the eastern wall. Four of them are on view today in the civic museum.

P. 4, l. 15
the great Tower: The Venetian fortress at the entrance to the harbor of Herakleion.

P. 6, l. 15
Ios, Sikinos, Serifos, Milos: Islands of the Cyclades group.

P. 7, l. 11
There the asparagus, there the kale: In keeping with the poet's advice, we have not always translated the flora and fauna of this poem literally, but with an eye to sound and tone, the values that controlled the poet's choice of terms in the Greek.

P. 7, l. 36
the Virgin's mare: Popular name of the praying mantis, *mantis religioso.*

P. 8, ll. 23–24
ROES . . . YELTIS: Anagrams of favorite motifs in Elytis's poetry, that is, Eros, Sea, Marina, Sun, Immortality, Elytis.

P. 12, l. 7
Saint Marina with the demons: According to folk tradition, Saint Marina has the power to liberate man from the demons that torment him.

P. 12, l. 9
the Island gulfed by olive groves: Lesbos, or Mytilini, the poet's ancestral home.

P. 12, ll. 11–12
He who gave his blood . . . of the Saint: The allusion is not to Christ but to an eighteenth-century martyr, Theodoros of Mytilini, placed by local tradition at the beginning of the poet's family tree.

P. 12, l. 15
Yera: A gulf of Lesbos surrounded by the five villages mentioned in the lines that follow. The ancestors of the poet's mother came from this district of the island.

P. 13, ll. 25–28
those who wear the black shirt . . . Neocondors: Characteristics and neologisms depicting the various "barbarians" who have invaded Greece.

P. 13, l. 30
Tetractys: Pythagorean figure (ten dots forming an equilateral triangle) representing the number 10 and showing its composition as 1+2+3+4. The later Pythagoreans regarded it as "holy," the heart of creation. .∴.

P. 14, ll. 4–5
the Upright Pillars . . . Knowledge of God: Vision of the Parthenon and its carved frieze.

"The Passion"
The form of this section consists of a pattern which includes the following three types or units: Psalms, in free verse (indicated by roman numerals); Odes, in various intricate but strict metrical stanzas (numbered alphabetically in lower case); Readings, in loosely rhythmical prose. Each Reading is surrounded by two Odes (O + R + O) and this again by four Psalms (PP + ORO + PP). The section is divided into three equal parts of identical binary pattern (PPOROPPOROPP). Where the parts join, the Psalms are four in a row instead of two. It should be noted that in the original text each Ode has its own metrical pattern (syllabic and accentual) which is repeated in every stanza. According to the poet's commentary, this formal arrangement corresponds to the following thematic structure:

   Part One: Consciousness Facing Tradition. The Vehicles of Freedom: Poet and Consciousness (Psalm I), and Poet and Language (Psalm II). Birth and sanction of the concepts Liberty and Language (Ode a), The Confrontation of Evil (First Reading), and Fortitude (Ode b), concepts which demand virtues such as Frugality (Psalm III) and Pride and Rebellion (Psalm IV), that is, the Pillars of the Native Land, with full awareness of the consequences, which are Solitude (Ode c), Struggle (Second Reading), and Sacrifice (Ode d) and which make the conscious man turn to deeper elements, that is, the Guardians of Tradition: The Mountain (Psalm V) and The Sea (Psalm VI).

   Part Two: Consciousness Facing Danger. The External Danger: The Enemy (Psalm VII) and The "Protectors" (Psalm VIII), who seek to alter human authenticity and lead to The Quest for the Soul (Ode e), The Heroic Deed (Third Reading), The Invocation of Justice (Ode f) and to the Intelligible Sun, so that the consciousness may rise over those who are The Erring Bourgeois (Psalm IX) and The Decadent Young (Psalm X), that is, The Internal Danger, and who constitute the image of the present world, which is made equally of Beauty and Misery (Ode g), Greatness and Martyrdom (Fourth Reading), and Elation and Tears (Ode h), the present world of perverted Western Christian civilization which must be exorcised by new weapons: The Gospel of Pure Water and Poetic Speech (Psalm XI) and the other Cross consisting of the Trident and the Dolphin (Psalm XII), that is, the Natural Greek Symbols.

   . *Part Three: Consciousness Surpassing Danger.* Physical Metaphysics: The Beatification of the Senses (Psalm XIII) and The Reinstatement of the Senses (Psalm XIV), which, for another future, emerge as Oracles from the Barren Rock (Ode i), Teachings from the Fires of Destruction (Fifth Reading), and Voices from the Blood of Love (Ode j), and which reach The Comparison with the Deity (Psalm XV) and The Denial of Fate (Psalm XVI), that is, The Surpassing of Death, through the vehicle of the one who is The Poet as Monk of Bodily Vigor (Ode k), The Poet as Modern Prophet (Sixth Reading), and The Poet as Evangelist of a Transcendental Country (Ode l), which is the present country reached after the fulfillment of the "void" of sacrifice and which has been realized through The Mutual Compensation of Good and Evil (Psalm XVII) and The Reidentification of Beauty and Justice (Psalm XVIII), that is, the Absolute Reality of the Spirit, Glory of the Poet and of Greece.

P. 17, l. 7
black shirts: The Italian fascists who invaded Greece in 1940.

P. 18, l. 25
Easter eggs cracking: According to a common Greek Orthodox custom, friends and relatives try to crack each other's colored eggs by striking the tip of one against the other.

P. 18, l. 28
the first words of the Hymn: The Greek National Anthem is based on the first four quatrains of "Hymn to Liberty" by Dionysios Solomos (1798–1857). The "'first words" (strictly speaking, the first two lines, with some alterations and omissions) are quoted by Elytis in the last line of the Ode that follows.

P. 19, l. 5
the L and the Y: The original has "the E and the L," which are the first two letters of at least three pertinent words: "Ellas" (Greece), "Eleftheria" (Liberty), and "Elytis." Our equivalent applies only to the latter two, which are predominant in this context.

P. 19, l. 18
"The terrible edge of your sword": Quotation from "Hymn to Liberty" by Solomos (see note to p. 18, l. 28 above).

P. 20, the title
"The March Toward the Front": The First Reading is based on the poet's own experience as a lieutenant in the Greek-Italian war of 1940–41.

P. 20, l. 4
Khimara to Tepeleni: Himarë and Tepelenë are cities in southern Albania (or northern Epirus) that were occupied by the counterattacking Greek forces in the Albanian campaign of 1940–41.

P. 21, ll. 29–30
"Oi, oi, mana mou": Intimate Greek exclamation of pain and grief, addressed to one's own mother, whether present or absent.

P. 26, the title
"The Mule Drivers": This Reading is also based on the poet's experiences in the Albanian campaign of 1940–41.

P. 26, l. 3
Délvino, Saints Saránda, Koritsá: Delvinë, Sarandë, and Korcë are cities of southern Albania (or northern Epirus) that were occupied by the counterattacking Greek forces in the Albanian campaign.

P. 26, l. 4
biscuits: Substituted, here and below, for the "halva" of the original, which might convey to the non-Greek reader a wrong impression of exotic and luxurious *delicatesse* rather than of meager rations.

P. 26, l. 16
Zois: common Greek name suggesting the word "zoi," life.

P. 26, ll. 17–18
the five-fingered sign: Traditional gesture (the palm, with fingers spread, thrust out at a person or an object) expressing contempt or disgust and casting a spell of blindness.

P. 26, l. 20
Lefteris: Demotic form of "Eleftherios," a common Greek name suggesting liberty.

P. 28, l. 5
Master Builder: The reference here is not to Ibsen's play but to a Greek folk ballad in which the construction of the bridge of Arta is achieved only by a human sacrifice: the Master Builder's wife has to be buried alive inside the bridge.

81

P. 29, l. 5
Pindos . . . Athos: Two mountains of Greece embodying respectively the heroic and the spiritual tradition.

P. 29, l. 13
by his heel: Probably a reference to Achilles.

P. 30, ll. 23–25
Saint Kanaris . . . Saint Manto: Constantine Kanaris, Andreas Miaoulis, and Manto Mavrogenis were among the naval leaders of the Greek War of Independence (1821–28). They are here sanctified by the poet.

P. 31, l. 22
not even a fairy's glance . . . their speech: According to Greek popular tradition, any man meeting a fairy must be careful not to speak to her; if he does, he will turn dumb.

P. 32, l. 3
the fowl of the North and the beasts of the East: An allusion to the Italian, German, and Bulgarian invaders of Greece during World War II. The "fowl" probably telescopes the rooster's feathers of the Italian Bersaglieri and the German eagle.

P. 34, the title
"The Great Sally": A chronicle of the first public demonstration of the Greek Resistance, which took place in Athens on March 25 (Day of National Independence), 1942. The demonstrators were mainly students and war invalids.

P. 34, l. 9
with swollen feet: Because of the famine caused by the German and Italian occupation and by the blockade of the Allies.

P. 35, l. 1
Intelligible: Not visible, but apprehensible by the intellect.

P. 36, l. 14
in the lairs of Lycabettus: A steep hill at the residential center of Athens. On its southern slopes the homes of many wealthy Greeks and foreign residents form the cosmopolitan quarter of Kolonaki, where the poet himself now lives.

P. 37, l. 1
the young Alexandrians: The original can mean either "new" or "young." We have chosen the latter in view of the poet's unpublished commentary, in which he states that he is referring to the "decadent, pseudomodern young, who do not believe in anything and proclaim false revolutions."

P. 38, l. 14
the son of Haggith: Adonijah, son of Haggith and elder brother of Solomon, was put to death by his brother for having asked to be given Abishag the Shunammite for his wife. See I Kings 2:13–25.

P. 39, the title
"The Vacant Lot with the Nettles": This Reading chronicles a typical event of the latter days of the German Occupation in Athens: the outskirts of the city were constantly raided by the SS in an attempt to repress by terror the growing Resistance Movement.

P. 39, l. 2
Lefteris's neighborhood: Obviously a poor, working-class neighborhood, probably inhabited by refugees who came from Asia Minor in 1922. Lefteris (whose name suggests the Greek word for liberty) is almost certainly the same person who appears in the Second Reading.

P. 39, l. 13
the Man with the Hood: During the raids mentioned above, the Nazis were usually accompanied by a local Greek traitor, whose face was covered by a hood showing only his eyes.

P. 39, l. 21
the Great Foreigner . . . collar: The SS officer in command of the raid.

P. 42, l. 4
Mavroyeni fountain: On the Aegean island of Paros there are several public fountains attributed to the bounty of the Mavroyeni family. The most beautiful of these is dated 1777 and is situated near the market, close to the home of Manto Mavroyeni (whose name was invoked in Psalm VI; see note to p. 30, ll. 23–25). One might add, however, "that the family of Mavroyeni, closely connected with Paros and Mykonos, rose to eminence among those Greeks who served the Ottoman Empire in many high offices" (Eric Forbes-Boyd, *Aegean Quest* [London, 1970], p. 177).

P. 42, l. 17
Seljuks: The Turkish nomadic tribes that founded the Ottoman Empire. The original offers an eccentric spelling of the word, perhaps meant to convey the irony of a "refined" modern version of these primitive and fierce warriors.

P. 42, l. 18
Chagans (or Hagans): Byzantine word for the leaders of barbarian hordes that invaded the Empire from the East.

P. 42, l. 23
Dionysios Solomos: the poet to whom Elytis alluded in Psalm II and whom he quoted in Ode a (see note to p. 18, l. 28).

P. 42, l. 24
Alexandros Papadiamantis: Famous novelist and short-story writer (1851–1911) from the island of Skiathos (northwest Aegean). His work depicts, with subtlety and tenderness, the traditional customs and beliefs of the islanders, seen from a realistic yet intensely spiritual perspective.

P. 43, ll. 28–29
strike the Trident . . . cross it with the dolphin: Many neoclassical fountains in Greece are decorated with a relief showing a trident entwined by a dolphin. Whatever the original symbolism of this emblem may have been, it now seems to escape the average Greek. Elytis here (and in Psalm XVII) is trying to reconstitute the symbol in terms of its natural components, as a substitute for the Christian cross (which he sees as a symbol of sacrifice).

P. 45, ll. 24–25
Maistros . . . Graigos: Northwest and northeast winds.

P. 47, the title
"The Courtyard of Lambs": The Fifth Reading is a parable based on the experiences of the Greek people during the Civil War that broke out after the liberation of Greece (1944) and went on intermittently until 1949.

P. 49, l. 1
purple: The Greek word for purple (used by Elytis as a verb) denotes a deep red color, a royal emblem, whereas the English conveys a shade between mauve and violet. We have tried to retain the image with as little distortion as possible.

P. 49, l. 4
Everlasting Rose: Traditional epithet for the Holy Virgin, with a pictorial counterpart in post-Byzantine icons.

P. 52, l. 17
Bucephalus: The legendary wild horse of Alexander the Great.

P. 53, l. 16
"Philips" and "Roberts": Names (the second most unusual in Greek) of "decadent" youths, according to the poet's commentary.

P. 53, l. 25
the colors of Hymmetus: This mountain has given Athens the name of the "violet-crowned city." In fact, the colors of Hymmetus vary considerably not only from season to season but also from hour to hour, and the famous violet is normally seen only for a few minutes, most clearly in winter at dusk.

P. 53, l. 26
Sikinos: An island of the Cyclades group.

P. 54, l. 2
Erechtheum: A temple on the Acropolis of Athens, famous for its colonnade of caryatids, that is, female figures used as columns to support the entablature.

P. 56, l. 11
The sign . . . dolphin: See the note to Psalm XII, p. 43, ll. 28–29.

P. 57, l. 9
Prince of Lilies: An allusion to the famous Minoan fresco in the Herakleion museum.

"The Gloria"
In the first edition of the Greek text, this section had the same title as the entire poem *("To Axion Esti"),* a circumstance which naturally caused some confusion, yet which also underlines the importance of this coda. Here again we have a strict formal pattern, though the lines are, as a rule, autonomous, and they are arranged into relatively simple groups of four, three, and two lines, sometimes loosely rhymed. The section is divided into three parts, of which the first and third are identical in structure: 6 quatrains + 1 triplet + 6 quatrains + 1 triplet + 5 quatrains + 7 couplets; the second part has a similar structure: 6 quatrains + 1 triplet + 6 quatrains + 1 triplet + 6 quatrains + 1 triplet + 5 quatrains + 7 couplets. Further metrical refinements, impossible to duplicate in translation, can be discerned in the original text. One should point out that the formal pattern of this section keeps it from degenerating into a random enumeration of things "worthy of praise." The triplets, for one, serve as thematic centers for the two quatrains that precede them, each time naming a different set of "basic species" (winds-islands; flowers-girls-ships; mountains-trees). Also, the couplets at the end of each part have a specific motif: in the first part, "hail" (addressed, according to the poet, "to the girl-child who will save the world and who personifies the poetic idea"); in the second part, "he" (which refers to the Poet); and in the third part, "Now" and "Forever" (the central motif of the poem).

P. 61, ll. 9–10
the Mermaid's hand/holding the schooner: Probably a reference to the popular Aegean iconography of the "Mermaid Madonna."

P. 62, ll. 5–7
Maistros . . . Tramountana: Popular names of winds, mainly used by seamen: Maistros (northwest), Levantes (east), Garbis (southwest), Pounentes (west), Graigos (northeast), Siroccos (southeast), Ostria (south), Tramountana (north).

P. 63, l. 9
the meltemi: Northern wind that appears in the eastern Mediterranean during the summer.

P. 63, ll. 13–15
Sifnos . . . Sikinos: Of the islands named here, Thasos is in the northeast Aegean; Sifnos, Amorgos, Santorini, Ios, and Sikinos belong to the Cyclades; Alonnisos to the northern Sporades; Ithaka to the Ionian Islands; Kos to the Dodekanese.

P. 63, l. 16
Myrto: The same name occurs in the Sixth Reading ("young Myrto, the whore from Sikinos") and again below, among the names of girls belonging to the poet's "personal mythology," as he phrases it in his commentary.

P. 64, l. 5
Hera of the tree's ancient trunk: An allusion to Hera's attributes of Mother Earth and goddess of fertility and vegetation.

P. 64, l. 8
Kyra-Penelope: A deliberately ambiguous reference to both the faithful royal wife of Odysseus and any modern peasant woman bearing the same name.

P. 64, ll. 13–14
remembrance day . . . Julitta: July 15. Probably a date connected with the poet's "personal mythology."

P. 65, l. 8
Serpent's belt of stars: The reference is to the constellation named Serpent.

P. 67, l. 10
Mnisareti: A girl depicted in a famous ancient tomb-relief, found in the Keramikos cemetery of Athens and now in the Munich Glyptothek.

P. 68, l. 2
Aretousa: Princess and beloved heroine of a popular Cretan romance of the seventeenth century, *Erotokritos,* by Vicenzos Kornaros.

P. 68, ll. 3–4
"descending . . . tunic": The original quotes a fragment of Sappho (see Lobel-Page, *Poetarum Lesbiorum Fragmenta* [Oxford, 1955], fr. 54, p. 39).

P. 68, ll. 13–15
Ersi . . . Cynthia: According to the poet, all these names of girls belong to his "personal mythology."

P. 68, l. 17
Arignota: A name probably derived from Sappho (*op. cit.,* fr. 96, p. 78), where it is used as an adjective meaning "well known."

P. 69, l. 14
Hyperboreans: According to ancient Greek mythology, a legendary people living "beyond the north," in a peaceful and blessed country where the sun rose and set once a year.

P. 69, l. 16
Evadne: The wife, "faithful unto death," of Capaneus, one of the seven legendary champions who marched against Thebes to vindicate the rights of Polynices, son of Oedipus, against his brother Eteocles.

P. 69, l. 16
Nicothoa: An obscure mythological figure, also known as Aello or Aellopous, one of the Harpies ("Snatchers"), marine monsters personifying violent winds that snatch people away.

85

P. 70, ll. 8–9

Marina . . . and the demons: See the notes to "The Genesis," p. 8, ll. 23–24 and p. 12, l. 7; also the triplet listing the girls of the poet's "personal mythology," p. 68, ll. 13–15.

P. 71, l. 11

the Ion: This can mean either "the man from Ionia" or "the man named Ion." The former must be excluded, because Lesbos (Elytis's home island) belongs to Aeolia and not to Ionia. The latter can be a reference to the mythical patriarch of the Ionians (the people inhabiting Athens, most of the Cyclades, and the central part of Asia Minor) about whom Euripides wrote a play, or to a versatile poet from Chios (fifth century B.C.), or even to the imaginary rhapsode who discusses poetry with Socrates in Plato's dialogue.

P. 72, l. 3

the nine steps that Plotinus climbed: An allusion to Plotinus's *Enneads,* so called because each book of this mystical work is divided into nine chapters, progressing from matter to soul, from soul to reason, and from reason to God.

P. 72, l. 4

the earthquake's chasm that filled with flowers: A direct quotation from Solomos (see notes to Psalm II, p. 18, l. 28, and Ode a, p. 19, l. 18).

P. 73, ll. 5–7

Pindus . . . Ainos: Of the mountains named here, Pindus, Parnassus, Olympus, Taygetus, and Athos are well known; less so, perhaps, are Rodopi (in Thrace), Tymphristos (on the northeast mainland), Dirfys (on the island of Euboea), and Ainos (on the island of Cephalonia).

P. 73, l. 19

Liyeri: Probably a reference to the folk song known as "Liyeri ston Adhi" (The Slender Girl in Hades). The girl in question begs to be raised to the upper world in order to see how her kin are grieving for her, only to learn that her kin are in fact not mourning for her but enjoying life as usual.

P. 75, l. 10

Heraclitus . . . voice: A reference to the fact that this philosopher's words survive only in fragments or aphoristic quotations.

OTHER BOOKS BY ODYSSEUS ELYTIS (in Greek)

Orientations
Sun the First
Heroic and Elegaic Song for the Lost Second Lieutenant of the Albanian Campaign
Six and One Remorses for the Sky
The Tree of Light and the Fourteenth Beauty
The Sovereign Sun
The Monogram
The "R"s of Eros
The Painter Theophilos
The Siblings

OTHER BOOKS BY THE TRANSLATORS

EDMUND KEELEY

The Libation
Six Poets of Modern Greece (with Philip Sherrard)
The Gold-Hatted Lover
Vassilis Vassilikos: The Plant, the Well, the Angel (with Mary Keeley)
George Seferis: Collected Poems, 1924–1955 (with Philip Sherrard)
The Impostor
C. P. Cavafy: Passions and Ancient Days (with George Savidis)
Modern Greek Writers (editor, with Peter Bien)
C. P. Cavafy: Selected Poems (with Philip Sherrard)
Voyage to a Dark Island
C. P. Cavafy: Collected Poems (with Philip Sherrard and George Savidis)

GEORGE SAVIDIS

For Seferis: A Symposium (editor)
C. P. Cavafy: Poems, 1886–1933 (editor)
Angelos Sikelianos: Lyric Life (editor)
The Editions of Cavafy, 1891–1932
K. G. Kariotakis: The Complete Poems (editor)
C. P. Cavafy: Unpublished Poems, 1882–1923 (editor)
A. Valaoritis: Photeinos (editor)
C. P. Cavafy: Passions and Ancient Days (with Edmund Keeley)
George Seferis: Poems (editor)
Against the Current
C. P. Cavafy: Collected Poems (with Edmund Keeley and Philip Sherrard)

PITT POETRY SERIES
Ed Ochester, General Editor

Milne Holton and Paul Vangelisti, eds., *The New Polish Poetry: A Bilingual Collection*
David Huddle, *Paper Boy*
Shirley Kaufman, *The Floor Keeps Turning*
Shirley Kaufman, *From One Life to Another*
Shirley Kaufman, *Gold Country*
Ted Kooser, *Sure Signs: New and Selected Poems*
Abba Kovner, *A Canopy in the Desert: Selected Poems*
Paul-Marie Lapointe, *The Terror of the Snows: Selected Poems*
Larry Levis, *Wrecking Crew*
Jim Lindsey, *In Lieu of Mecca*
Tom Lowenstein, tr., *Eskimo Poems from Canada and Greenland*
Archibald MacLeish, *The Great American Fourth of July Parade*
Peter Meinke, *The Night Train and The Golden Bird*
Judith Minty, *In the Presence of Mothers*
James Moore, *The New Body*
Carol Muske, *Camouflage*
Leonard Nathan, *Dear Blood*
Sharon Olds, *Satan Says*
Gregory Pape, *Border Crossings*
Thomas Rabbitt, *Exile*
Belle Randall, *101 Different Ways of Playing Solitaire and Other Poems*
Ed Roberson, *Etai-Eken*
Ed Roberson, *When Thy King Is A Boy*
Eugene Ruggles, *The Lifeguard in the Snow*
Dennis Scott, *Uncle Time*
Herbert Scott, *Groceries*
Richard Shelton, *The Bus to Veracruz*
Richard Shelton, *Of All the Dirty Words*
Richard Shelton, *You Can't Have Everything*
Gary Soto, *The Elements of San Joaquin*
Gary Soto, *The Tale of Sunlight*
David Steingass, *American Handbook*
David Steingass, *Body Compass*
Tomas Tranströmer, *Windows & Stones: Selected Poems*
Alberta T. Turner, *Learning to Count*
Alberta T. Turner, *Lid and Spoon*
Constance Urdang, *The Lone Woman and Others*
Cary Waterman, *The Salamander Migration and Other Poems*
Marc Weber, *48 Small Poems*
Bruce Weigl, *A Romance*
David P. Young, *The Names of a Hare in English*
David P. Young, *Sweating Out the Winter*